≈≈≈≈≈≈≈

DERELICTION OF DUTY
AND
THE RISE OF PSYCHOLOGY

AS REFLECTED IN THE "CASE" OF CONRAD'S *LORD JIM*

Greg Mogenson

A publication of
The International Society for Psychology as the Discipline of Interiority
Monograph Series, vol. I

Cover Design: Michael Mendis

Cover Painting by H. C. Hensley

ISBN-10: 1979133603
ISBN-13: 978-1979133609

SOURCES AND ABBREVIATIONS

The following abbreviations have been used for frequently cited sources:

Lord Jim: Joseph Conrad, *Lord Jim*, Cedric Watts & Robert Hampson, eds., London: Penguin Books, 1986. Cited by page number.

CEP: Wolfgang Giegerich, *The Collected English Papers of Wolfgang Giegerich*, 6 vols., New Orleans: Spring Journal Books, 2005-2013. Cited by volume and page number.

CW: Carl Gustav Jung, *Collected Works*, 20 vols. Herbert Read, Michael Fordham, Gerhard Adler and William McGuire, eds., R. F. C. Hull, trans., Princeton: Princeton University Press, 1957-1979. Cited by volume and paragraph number.

Table of Contents

ACKNOWLEDGEMENTS

A shorter version of this essay was presented as a talk at a conference of The International Society for Psychology as the Discipline of Interiority that was held at the Serra Retreat, Malibu, California, May 12-14, 2016. The main difference between that earlier talk and the present text is that I here offer, in lieu of an accompanying seminar, extensive endnotes touching upon many topics and subject matters of importance to analytical psychology in general, and to psychology as discipline of interiority, in particular. With gratitude for a warm reception and incisive questions, I want to thank the attendees of that conference, which was dedicated to the theme of "Interiority, Truth, and Psychology." For further collegial support along the way, I wish also to thank Rita Mendis-Mogenson, Wolfgang Giegerich, Daniel Anderson, John Hoedl, Colleen Hendrick, Santo Tarantino, Peter White, and Michael Mendis.

G.M.

> It seemed to me I was being made to comprehend
> the Inconceivable ... made to look at the convention
> that lurks in all truth and on the essential sincerity of
> falsehood. ... The occasion was obscure,
> insignificant ... : a lost youngster, one in a million—
> but then he was one of us; an incident as completely
> devoid of importance as the flooding of an ant-heap,
> and yet the mystery of his attitude got hold of me as
> though he had been an individual in the forefront of
> his kind, as if the obscure truth involved were
> momentous enough to affect mankind's conception
> of itself ...[1]

> Captain Marlow speaking of Jim

LITERATURE AS THE OTHER OF PSYCHOLOGY

This essay is about the speculative confluence of psychology and literature. More specifically, and leaving the separateness of these different disciplines behind, it is about the speculative turn that psychology might take when meeting itself in great works of literature. In 1900—that is, in the very year that saw the publication of Freud's *The Interpretation of Dreams*—Joseph Conrad published *Lord Jim*, one of his finest novels. No less psychological in its scope than the writings of Freud were literary in their style (Freud, it will be recalled, was later awarded the Goethe Prize for Literature), Conrad's novel may with equal felicity be likened to a lengthy case study. For just as the originator of psychoanalysis wrote short story and even novel-like accounts of such characters as Dora and Little Hans,[2] so Conrad wrote a case study-like novel about a character he called Jim. But how different Conrad's psychoanalysis of Jim is from Freud's analysis of his characters! And on the theoretical level, too, how different the psychoanalysis that would learn of itself from its share in the fate of this literary character! Usually, the contribution that psychoanalysis makes with respect to literary criticism is a one-way street. Insights from the clinic are applied ready-made to some aspect of a literary work. The speculative psychoanalysis I shall be pursuing here, however, has rather to do with how psychology or "the soul"[3] re-definitionally comes home to itself through such topics and subject matters as the genre of the novel, generally, or some instance of novelistic art, in particular. Just as Jung regarded mythology, religion, and medieval alchemy, each in their own way, as "the other" of his analytical psychology, so we may regard *Lord Jim* that way to, as "the other" of that speculative turn in analytical psychology which has come to be known as the discipline of interiority.[4]

To begin with I want to give the principal character of Conrad's novel a thematizing, psychoanalytic name. Just as the protagonists in two of Freud's major clinical papers were dubbed by him the "Wolf Man" and the "Rat Man" respectively, and just as a patient Jung wrote of has subsequently come to be known as "the Solar Phallus Man,"[5] so may Jim, the young chief mate in this novel of the sea, be referred to for our purposes as "The Disgraced Ship's Officer."

Briefly summarized, the story is as follows. An old, rust-eaten cargo steamer is voyaging across the Indian Ocean to the Red Sea with the purpose of transporting eight-hundred Moslem pilgrims to their holy places. One night during the course of this crossing calamity strikes. The steamer lurches in the water, possibly because it has collided with some sort of obstruction, such as a water-logged wreck or sunken derelict. To the captain and the officers on watch, disaster seems imminent. The hull of the *Patna*, as their ship is called, appears to have been breached. In a moment or two, when this rupture widens, the ship will in all likelihood be immediately swallowed under by the sea. And it is here, precisely in this lurch, that Disgrace enters the picture. Without alerting the passengers (for what a riot there would be if they were to awaken all at once) the skipper, a few of his officers, and our protagonist, Jim, abandon their responsibilities and take to a lifeboat. Only later do they discover, after being rescued by a passing ship, that their vessel did not come to the dire end from which they had selfishly acted to save themselves, but was also rescued and towed to safety. With this revelation, the disgrace of having abandoned ship is redoubled and then some. Explanations, the deserters realize, are sure to be demanded. As professional seamen entrusted with the welfare of a ship and its cargo, they will be hauled up before a mariner's inquest to answer for their actions. Not wanting to face up to this, however, the skipper and two of the other officers very quickly make scarce. Departing at their first opportunity, each to a haven of his own, it is quite as if they again took to lifeboats in dereliction of their duties. Jim alone, the most junior of the lot, remains. Resolutely determined to live down the seeming cowardliness of the actions he was drawn into, he will not forsake the duty he has subsequently been charged with of giving his testimony at the inquest, even though this will most certainly entail humiliation for him personally and very likely the sinking of his career as well.

And what was the outcome of Jim's decision to stay? Before turning to this topic, which is what the rest of the novel is mainly about, I must first introduce another character. Besides the disgraced, and yet in the sense just described, still stalwart Jim, the other main character of the novel is the dignified and in some ways fatherly Captain Marlow. An attendee at Jim's trial, Marlow is a captain in the merchant marine who has taken an interest in Jim's case and character. Not only does he attend the inquest looking into the *Patna* affair, as it notoriously came to be known, he also lends an ear to the young ship's mate when the two of them dine together over the course of a long evening, gaining in this way both a fuller account of the fiasco that had led to Jim's misconduct and a deeper sense of the mettle of this young man who, though "one of us,"[6] as Marlow repeatedly states, must thenceforth deal with his having, in the eyes of most men, if not finally of Marlow, sunk beneath the *niveau* of being worthy of such fellowship. And here, if I may, I would already like to add that it is this keen, supportive, and yet by no means uncritical interest of Marlow's that allows us to regard him as a literary precursor of what later in the century was to become the figure of the analyst even as, in a complimentary manner, Jim may be regarded as a literary precursor of the figure of the analysand or patient.

But let us continue with our *précis* of the novel. After the inquest, which sadly for Jim results in his being stripped of his credentials as a professional seaman, Marlow steers him toward a dock-side employment opportunity with a trading company in another port city. This he does out of concern for the young man and from worry over what now will become of him. While not condoning the actions that led to Jim's disgrace (Marlow is as appalled as the next fellow by Jim's dereliction of his duty), a friendly compassion has nevertheless been quickened within him. His kindness, however (as I have already intimated), has also another motive. As much a student of the human soul as he is the captain of a ship, Marlow's abiding interest is to study how Jim will thenceforth come to terms with his difficult fate. There will not be much to study, however, if the disgraced young man is not able to find a way of making his livelihood. Which is why Marlow directs him to a job prospect and writes a letter of introduction on his behalf.

So much for our first meeting with Captain Marlow and for his first contacts with Jim. The other context in which we meet up with him is as the teller of Jim's story. The bulk of the novel consists of Marlow telling the story of Jim's initial calamity and subsequent career to a group of his sea-faring cronies over the course of a long evening. It is a remarkable scene, already and in its own right, quite apart from its narrative content. A gifted raconteur, Marlow's account of Jim is given "after dinner, on a verandah … *in the deep dusk speckled by fiery cigar-ends.*"[7] A wonderful image! Deeply poetic, and psychological, too! Coming upon it the reader may be put in mind of similar imagery which has been discussed by Jung. When the psyche wishes to out-picture itself to itself as composed of multiple centres of consciousness it does so, according to Jung, by showing star-strewn night skies, the luminous eyes of schooling fish, and in another image, boat-lanterns of a regatta swaying against the darkness of a night sea.[8] Surely Conrad's image of "the deep dusk speckled by fiery cigar-ends" can readily be added to this list. But let us read on. Continuing the description of the setting in which Marlow recounts what he has learned of Jim, the novel's narrator tells of how "The elongated bulk of each cane-chair harboured a silent listener," and of how, since each of these puffed a cigar as he listened, "Now and then a small red glow would ... light up the fingers of a languid hand ... [and] flash a crimson gleam into a pair of pensive eyes overshadowed by a fragment of unruffled forehead ..." And what description, complimentary to this, is given of the story-teller, Marlow, himself? How is he depicted? From "the very first word uttered," we are told, "Marlow's body, extended at rest in the seat, would become very still [as he spoke], as though his spirit had winged its way back into the lapse of time and were speaking through his lips from the past."[9]

I will only note in passing the likeness of this description of Marlow's story-telling spirit to Hegel's famous description of philosophy as being like the owl of Minerva that only flies at dusk.[10] Just as Hegel regarded philosophy as the dusk-born afterthought in which its own age is comprehended, so we soon learn that Marlow's dusk-told story of Jim is a psychological version of the same. For when spoken of by a spirit of telling that, having "winged its way back into the lapse of time," speaks, as it were, through "lips from the past," Jim is discussed, not as a particular character who has such and such a personal psychology, but as an exemplary man at the transit point of one age or epoch to another. This, his universality, is made clear very early in Marlow's narrative. Though the mariner's inquest was officially about "How the *Patna* came by her hurt," "the court [we are told] did not expect to find [this] out; and in the whole audience there was not a man who cared."[11] For the interest that the case held was of an entirely different kind. As Marlow stipulates, "Whether they knew it or not the interest that drew [all the sailors in the port and all the waterside workers, too] ... was purely psychological—the expectation of some essential disclosure as to the strength, the power, the horror of human emotions."[12] But though this was what the inquest was more deeply and truly about for all in attendance, its official aims were more practical and limited. Though Jim stood ready to expose his soul to the most serious questions, "the questions put to him necessarily led him away from what … would have been the only truth worth knowing [due to their limited scope]."[13] As Marlow with respect to this wryly observes, "You can't expect the constituted authorities to inquire into the state of a man's soul—or is it only his liver?"[14] But if such an aim were out of reach for the inquest, this only meant that it became Marlow's task to continue to look into this subject matter. And so it was that by corresponding with Jim by letter, by visiting with him whenever he could, and by discussing his case with whoever shared his interest in it,[15] he continued to inquire into the state of this disgraced young ship officer's soul.

PRESENTING PROBLEM

I said that Marlow and Jim may be regarded as literary precursors of those protagonists of the subsequent psychological culture which were emergent at the time of this novel's publication, the analyst and patient. Following up upon this comparison—indulging in it, even, as the inevitable conceit of our reading (for we are psychologists, after all, and in the spirit of what in the hermeneutics of Gadamer is called *applicatio*[16] are bound to be reminded of experiences from our own practices when hearing tell of Jim!)—let us now take a closer look at this proto-patient and at what might already in advance of itself be called his presenting problem.

When Marlow first lay eyes upon Jim he was taken aback by the young man's nonchalant demeanor. Spotting him a few days before the inquest, "He looked [to the good captain] as unconcerned and unapproachable as only the young can look."[17] Also disconcerting for Marlow was how hale and hearty the young sailor seemed. "There he stood, clean-limbed, clean-faced, firm on his feet, as promising a boy as the sun ever shone on; and looking at him, knowing all he knew and a little more too, I was angry as if I had detected him trying to get something out of me by false pretenses. He had no business to look so sound. I thought to myself—well, if this sort can go wrong like that . . ."[18] An ellipsis at this point invites the reader to finish the Captain's thought: "If this sort can go wrong, *then anyone can!*" Continuing more colourfully Marlow then adds: "and I felt as though I could fling down my hat and dance on it from sheer mortification, as I once saw the skipper of an Italian barque do because his duffer of a mate got into a mess with his anchors when making a flying moor in a roadstead full of ships."[19] Jim has made a mess of his life and on first impressions (though, of course, the truth is otherwise) gives the impression of not caring. Before the bar of human decency, this is abominable, and Marlow will feel the shame, the mortification, if this disgraced young sailor will not.

Now surely this is a familiar reaction. As analysts and psycho-therapists, we know something of the feelings Marlow describes from experiences with our own patients. Though we may not get as emotional as he did, having learned to work with such resistances when we come across them in our patients and in ourselves, we too know what it is to have our sympathies played upon by an analysand or patient who wittingly or unwittingly "tr[ies] to get something out of [us] by false pretences." And then, of course, our own proneness to identification may also figure into the mix, as when, for example, some quality or experience of the patient resonates with something akin to it in ourselves. If Marlow were an analyst-in-training, and not the character of a novel, we might happily direct him to the statement of Jung's from *The Psychology of the Transference*: "unless we prefer to be made fools of by our illusions, we shall, by carefully analyzing every fascination, extract from it a portion of our own personality, like a quintessence, and slowly come to recognize that we meet ourselves time and again in a thousand disguises on the path of life."[20] But Conrad's *Lord Jim* is already this insight of Jung's a half-century before Jung was able to state it in this form![21] And here now, taking a little further my conceit of seeing Marlow and Jim as forerunners of what later in our history became the analyst and patient, I might as well add that, just as on the very next page of the novel the Captain speaks of his being reminded by the sight of Jim of the many young sailors he had schooled in the ways of the sea, so might we while reading of this remember the various patients and analysands over the years who got their sea legs in our offices, remembering at the same time the analysts and clinical supervisors in whose offices we, like young Jims ourselves, got ours!

> The sea has been good to me, but when I remember all these boys who passed through my hands, some grown up now and some drowned by this time, but all good stuff for the sea, I don't think I have done badly by it either. Were I to go home to-morrow, I bet that before two days passed over my head some sunburnt young chief mate would overtake me at some dock gateway or other, and a fresh deep voice speaking above my hat would ask: "Don't you remember me, sir? Why! little So-and-so. Such and such a ship. It was my first voyage." And I would remember a bewildered little shaver, no bigger than the back of this chair, with a mother and perhaps a big sister on the quay, very quiet but too upset to waive their handkerchiefs at the ship that glides out gently between the pier-heads …[22]

After this aside let us return to the theme of this section. It is in Marlow's account of his first sighting of Jim that we get our first glimpse of what, with anachronistic intent, I am calling "the presenting problem" of their proto-psychoanalysis. Jim, as we know, had disgraced himself as a chief ship's mate by dishonourably abandoning the *Patna*. Marlow, of course, is already aware of this before their first meeting. Which is why Jim's hands-in-his-pockets, nonchalance so angers him. The contrast is just too odious. Why, the sheer effrontery of his looking like that! Has the young sailor no shame?! Also of concern to Marlow is the doubt that Jim's appearance casts upon Marlow's own competency as a judge in such matters of character. For, as he is troubled to realize, even though his eye is jaundiced by knowledge of the young man's failure, he still has the impression of Jim as being every inch a sailor.

> ... he was outwardly so typical of that good, stupid kind we like to feel marching left and right of us in life, of the kind that is not disturbed by the vagaries of intelligence and the perversions of—of nerves, let us say. He was the kind of fellow you would, on the strength of his looks, leave in charge of the deck—figuratively and professionally speaking. I say I would, and I ought to know. Haven't I turned out youngsters enough in my time, for the service of the Red Rag, to the craft of the sea, to the craft whose whole secret could be expressed in one short sentence, and yet must be driven afresh every day into young heads till it becomes the component part of every waking thought, till it is present in every dream of their young sleep![23]

Though Marlow does not explicitly say what the secret is upon which the craft of the sea (or we might add: the craft of any profession) depended at that time, it is clear enough from the immediate context of these lines and from the novel as a whole. As before with the ellipsis we discussed above, the reader must supply this for himself:

DO YOUR DUTY!

ACT IN ACCORANCE WITH THE HIGHEST STANDARD OF PROFESSIONAL CONDUCT!

FULFILL YOUR PLACE IN THE ORDER OF THINGS!

However we word it, this is the secret, i.e., the intangible, and yet indispensable master ingredient, that "must be driven afresh every day into young heads till it becomes the component part of every waking thought ..." But here is the rub. Jim's worthiness as the subject of the interest that has so widely been taken in him resides in his evident unworthiness. It is only because he failed in the sphere of duty, which has the status of a universal, that everyone in the port and who makes their life by the sea has taken an interest in his case. And this is also what interested the intelligent and serious-minded Marlow. As he puts it himself,

> Why I longed to go grubbing into the deplorable details of an occurrence which, after all, concerned me no more than as a member of an obscure body of men held together by a community of inglorious toil and by fidelity to a certain standard of conduct, I can't explain. You may call it an unhealthy curiosity if you like; but I have a distinct notion I wished to find something. Perhaps, unconsciously, I hoped I would find that something, some profound and redeeming cause, some merciful explanation, some convincing shadow of an excuse. I see well enough now that I hoped for the impossible—for the laying of what is the most obstinate ghost of man's creation, of the uneasy doubt uprising like a mist, secret and gnawing like a worm, and more chilling than the certitude of death—the doubt of the sovereign power enthroned in a fixed standard of conduct.[24]

In this passage, the inception of psychology from out of the decline of duty is succinctly conveyed. Marlow, as he puts it, wants to defeat that "most obstinate ghost of man's [not God's!] creation," "the doubt … [that has negated] the sovereign power enthroned in a fixed standard of conduct." He wants to counter this by coming up with some "redeeming cause," "merciful explanation," "convincing shadow of an excuse." Something of the order, perhaps, of the psychoanalytic insights that Freud came up with when he wrote about those patients, in his words, who are "wrecked by success."[25] But this, as he concedes, was hoping for the impossible. Such nascent psychological efforts cannot redeem or shore up Tradition and its sense of Duty; they are rather its successor. There was nothing for it, then, but that Marlow follow up upon Jim's subsequent career, even as, giving the good captain something to follow up upon, Jim in that subsequent career inaugurates a truer sense of psychology than Marlow at first aimed for by contending with the negation which his disgrace has tasked him with. How will this disgraced young ship's officer become capable of his fate? This is what Marlow undertakes to know. Each day in our practices it is also what the Marlow in us is determined to discover. And the same goes with respect to those scandals reported in the wider world that strike a chord within us. As students of destinies that might have also been our own, these too prove often to be as compelling for us as Jim was for Marlow.[26]

HOIST ON HIS OWN PETARD

So far, we have been examining what I am calling the presenting problem of this literary proto-psychoanalysis from its analyst's, that is, from Marlow's vantage point. Turning now to Jim's side of the matter, we soon learn from the fuller description we are subsequently given that he was by no means as indifferent as he had initially seemed. On the contrary, the young ship's officer was as deeply concerned over his failure as anyone could possibly be, and on top of this, vexed with bewilderment about how it had come to pass that he had failed in his duty. How could he who was filled with little else than heroic intentions, and who had so keenly longed to be tested by whatever the life of the sea had in store for him, miscarry so shamefully? He would have liked to delve into this question himself, to have provided a long and detailed account.[27] But the psychology that might have been discovered in this way would have to wait upon another theorist. The inquest, as I mentioned, did not allow for any going into that. It simply measured Jim against the standard of conduct that sailors were then expected to live by and found him wanting. This is not to say, however, that the unsympathetic decision it made against Jim gave no traction to psychology at all. It is rather the other way around. As heir to and sequel of the literature that preceded it, psychology's provenance is owed in no small measure to accounts such as the present one of the disgraced Jim's erstwhile attempt to master his fate as disgraced one. For as we shall see, the Jim character's singular significance and universal merit resides in the exemplary and yet individual manner of his having embraced that exile from the soul that was already the beginning of its successor or *ersatz* form, psychology.[28] Or to put it another way, though Jim certainly failed in his duty, his dutifully facing up to this—at the inquest and thereafter in his subsequent life as an ethical subject— reflects the transformation of Duty[29] from what it had traditionally meant and involved. And it does this, moreover, in such a way that what Jung would later call "the individuation process" is richly anticipated.

But here, now, in speaking already about Jim's presenting problem as mediating the advent of the psychology that was born from the demise of Tradition, in general, and Duty, in particular, I am getting ahead of myself. In its initial stages, a presenting problem does not impress its bearer as being the first immediacy of his or her own cure. It is suffered, rather, ego-dystonically as painful or irksome symptoms. In Jim's case, this symptomatic suffering took the form of his being very sensitive to, and easily enraged by, any insinuation that he is a coward. If comments were made that touched upon this complex, if his nose was in some way rubbed in his having been disgraced as a sailor, he would become vexed to the point of violent irruption. In an early scene of the novel, for example, an obvious symbol of cowardice appears in the figure of a yellow dog. When someone calls out, "look at the wretched cur," Jim rounds upon Marlow, thinking the good captain has mocked him. "'I will allow no man,' … he murmured threateningly."[30] Fortunately for Marlow he is able to defuse the situation and get Jim to realize that the offending words did not have their source in him. Jim, however, remains adamant, and lastingly so: he will not let any man call him such names outside the courtroom situation. But then what is to be done? On the one hand, Jim will not let himself be mocked or chastised; on the other, he is highly prone to construing what he half-hears as just that, mockery and chastisement. If he is not to become a mad dog he will have to come up with some way to deal with this complex more civilly. And so it is that Jim, dodging the truth that his character in the novel mediates for his times (and, yet, engaging it at the same time in the way he stands up for himself in the aftermath of his disgrace[31]), adopts the avoidance strategy of moving from port to port and job to job as soon as it seems to him that his reputation has caught up with him. It was a compulsive and repetitive pattern. Although Jim readily distinguishes himself as an invaluable employee in each of the situations he is able subsequently to secure for himself, as if abandoning ship all over again, he abruptly and in all haste, moves on to more and more remote outposts whenever someone appears that might know his name and connect him to the *Patna* case.[32]

A BREACH IN THE HULL OF THE *PATNA*, A RUPTURE IN THE SOUL

We already know that the questions that were put to Jim at the mariner's inquest were intended only to ascertain the technical and procedural aspects of how the *Patna* came to be stranded in her peril. As such, they did not allow for the kind of soul-reckoning answers that Jim himself, no less than the others that took an interest in his testimony, was searching for and which the novel as a whole is ultimately about. In this section, pushing off from the inquest's too-limited focus, we shall be looking into the question of what the event which the *Patna* case is built around reflects with respect to the soul of its time.

But first a brief comment on methodology. In a lengthy interpretive treatise, Jung once declared that "the *tertium comparationis* for all these symbols is the libido, and the unity of meaning lies in the fact that they are all analogies for the same thing."[33] By this he meant that the various fantasy images produced by the patient whose material he was analyzing reflected the development and transformation of her libido, or as he also called this, her psychic energy. Similar to this stance, though only in formal regards, our interest in what follows will be focussed upon what the figures and events depicted in *Lord Jim* show with respect to the logic of Man's world-relation at their particular historical juncture, or to what is referred to in the literature of our discipline as the soul's logical life.[34] Just as, according to another statement of Jung's, "In myths and fairytales, as in dreams, the soul speaks about itself … ,"[35] so also does what might variously be called consciousness, mindedness, or "the soul" speak of itself in the pages of our novel.

Now if this be so we need only listen with a soulful ear to Jim's account of his being immediately undone as a sailor by the sight of the water-filled bulkheads of the *Patna's* breached hull to get to the heart of the matter which is the meaning of the novel. And what is this heart, this meaning? This can be stated without further ado. Since the *tertium comparationis* of every event and character of the novel is "the soul" (as indeed it must be for us given that we are psychologists), what Jim beholds when he comes upon the breach in the hull of the *Patna*, and what he further exemplifies through his failure to act in this circumstance in a manner that is fully in accordance with his concept as a sailor, can only be *the rupture in the soul itself!*

But what does it mean "rupture in the soul"? Many pertinent amplifications of this phrase could be cited. I will mention only one, a single sentence from a text of Jung's that I once underlined with what even then was arguably the same pencil stroke that I much later inscribed below those sentences of our novel in which Marlow speaks with chagrin of his futile wish to find an excuse for Jim that would serve at the same time to lay to rest that "ghost of doubt," as he aptly calls it, which had undermined his tradition's time-honoured belief in "… the sovereign power enthroned in a fixed standard of conduct."[36] In a letter written to Fr. Victor White a mere half-century after Conrad's *Lord Jim* was published, the great psychologist declares: "We are actually living in the time of the splitting of the world and the invalidation of Christ."[37] A radical statement! Drawing freely from the tropes of our novel, we could even characterize it as a hull-breaching, ship-splitting insight! But let me spell this out. What Jung calls "the splitting of the world and the invalidation of Christ," and what Conrad calls the obstinate doubt that in a ghostly fashion has torn asunder our belief in a sovereign power enthroned in a fixed standard of conduct, are but different expressions for the same soul-situation. There was a time when God was in his heaven and Christ a valid symbol, a time when Western man was provided for by these in metaphysical regards and there was a corresponding standard of conduct in all aspects of human life and society, a time when monarchs reigned and mimetic to this the people were backed up by the dignity of their various offices, here a captain, there a ship's mate—*a time, in short, when we lived in the soul so completely that there was as yet no psychological problem, and a time after this when for the first time there was.*[38] No wonder, then, that the young chief ship's mate, Jim, failed in his duty! Its *foundations* had changed. And no wonder as well that thenceforth the coming-of-age of the latter day Jims of our more determinately psychological times must navigate in the breached vessels of their own lives the individuating passage from a spiritless condition that appears to have nothing to serve to a new sensibility that serves at the pleasure of a nothing which is not merely or sheerly nothing, but the logically negative *result* of the Tradition that has in its demise gone under into it.[39]

"When your ship fails you," reflects Marlow, "your whole world seems to fail you; the world that made you, restrained you, took care of you." A line later he continues, "Of course, as with belief, thought, love, hate, conviction, or even the visual aspect of material things, there are as many shipwrecks as there are men..."[40] The "ship" that failed in Jim's case turned out not to be the *Patna* (which ultimately did not sink), but that of a venerable ideal of conduct.

FROM SAIL TO STEAM AND GOLD TO BRASS

I just distinguished between a time when Tradition reigned supreme and provided for everything and a time afterward when this was no longer the case and men like the disgraced chief ship's mate Jim became possible for the first time.[41] Commencing with the Enlightenment, this later time period extended all the way into the middle decades of the Nineteenth Century, that is, into the very time in which Conrad himself worked as a seaman and in which his novel is set. Now this latest time-period, it is important to note, was also the time of the Industrial Revolution. Indicative of this, the *Patna* is described as a steamship made of rusting iron. Why, it could even be said, *pars pro toto*, that the Industrial age as a whole is figured in the novel *as* this rusty steamer. So here already is the world-splitting, soul-rupturing tear in time that the breach in the *Patna* reflects.

Whereas, previously, when God was in his heaven and Tradition was sacrosanct, majestic sailing ships of baroque beauty sailed the seven seas and every sailor was like an angel at his station, Conrad's novel is set in the mechanistic times of serial production and alienation that followed afterward.[42] And here I should hasten to add that the epithet "godless" is also to be set in front of these subsequent times, for as novels of the sea go, *Lord Jim* is an especially godless one. We have only to compare it to Melville's *Moby Dick* to measure the extent of this. And yet, as a place-holder of the absent God, we have in its pages a reference to the *Patna's* cargo of eight-hundred Moslem pilgrims and to the prayer offered at the outset of the voyage by their turbaned Arab leader. But even as this prayer is being offered "a screwball lighthouse, planted by unbelievers on a treacherous shoal, seemed to wink ... its eye of flame, as if in derision of [the *Patna's*] errand of faith."[43] Why, it is quite as if that line from a Dostoyevsky novel of roughly the same period—"If God does not exist, everything is permitted"[44]—had proved itself with the new steam technology. Whereas previously the great sailing ships had needed God as much as they needed the wind, steamships such as the *Patna* had released themselves from both. Perhaps this is why, when at the height of his calamity the vexed skipper succumbs to cursing, he does not take the Lord's name in vain, but merely mutters "confounded steam! ... infernal steam!"[45]

The point to be grasped is that the giving way of sail to steam that occurred during the Eighteenth and Nineteenth centuries was indicative of that aforementioned Enlightenment period of soul-rupturing transition wherein "the world to which the known religions were answers ... moved out from under them,"[46] as Giegerich has aptly put it. Seen from within, that is, via the acuity of Conrad's literary vision, the world-splitting, soul-rupturing character of this period is depicted as the *Patna* having collided with what is likely a sunken derelict, on the one hand,[47] and by Jim's standing spellbound at the sight of the breach this has made in her hull, on the other.[48] But that is not all. Besides Jim's description of the *Patna's* wound there are in the novel at least two other depictions of this fraught moment in the soul's life. Turning to the first of these (as to what Jung in our quote from him on symbols called "analogies for the same thing"), let us rise to the insight that the rupture in the soul that is apperceived by Jim as the breach in the rusting hull of the *Patna* (and which was widened enormously by his subsequently abandoning ship!) is at the same time apperceived by Marlow as the disillusionment he is subject to when he first lays eyes on Jim. I again refer to the Captain's being affronted by Jim's looking so able and at ease after having behaved in such a disgraceful manner. Gazing upon this discrepancy as upon a split running through the world of those times, he is shocked to realize, as he puts it, that "I would have trusted the deck to that youngster on the strength of a single glance, and gone to sleep with both eyes—and, by Jove! *it wouldn't have been safe.*"[49] Brooding upon this he then immediately adds, "There are depths of horror in that thought. He [Jim] looked as genuine as a new sovereign, but there was some infernal alloy in his metal. How much? The least thing—the least drop of something rare and accursed; the least drop!—but he made you—standing there with his don't-care-hang-air—he made you wonder whether perchance he was nothing more rare than brass."[50] What we are calling the rupture in the soul is here the difference between the new sovereign-like character of a sailor who fully accords with his concept and that same sailor as not in accord with that at all, but owing to a minute drop of something rare and accursed, having the common character of brass. Now, of course, what Marlow here compares to brass has gone on in the psychoanalysis that was subsequently developed by Freud to be fully analyzed. "Three Essays on Sexuality," "Some Character Types met with in Psycho-Analysis": we have only to think of such papers as these to get the assay of this human-all-too-human metal. The psychoanalysis that the novel actually prefigures, however, is very differently oriented, very differently conceived. Rather than concentrating on the accursed drop and basing a reductive approach to interpretation upon a positivistic conception of its impurity as an "infernal alloy," the novel takes the appearance of this drop that Marlow is morally sickened to have spotted in the disgraced figure of Jim as the mediator of the soul's own self-negation. This is not to say that Marlow did not want to "see [Jim] squirm for [defaulting on] the honour of the [sailor's] craft."[51] That he wanted this is true enough, as his occasional barbed comments to Jim make clear. But there is a greater subject matter in the novel than the mettle and character of the disgraced Jim. Why, it could even be said that Marlow's interest in this young sailor's downfall and subsequent fate is only the conceit employed in the novel to study the form-change that *"the soul"* in a more universal sense passed through in moving from the times of its being metaphysically and religiously backed-up to the times that followed afterwards in which the soul-dignity it had had in these was objectively lost.[52]

CAPTAIN BRIERLY'S SUICIDE, THE DEATH OF AN IDEAL

So much for Jim's unwittingly having apperceived the rupture in the soul as a breach in the rusty hull of the *Patna* and for Marlow's having apperceived it as the infernal alloy which is odiously obscured, and yet, obscenely revealed, by Jim's continuing, even in the immediate aftermath of his disgrace, to look like a newly minted sovereign. Let us now turn to another depiction, another sighting. Early in the novel we briefly meet with a character who is precisely the opposite of a disgraced ship's officer. I refer to the high-ranking captain who at first gives the impression of being "consumedly bored by the honour thrust upon him"[53] of serving on the panel of the inquest—the impeccable Captain Brierly. Now I say the *impeccable* Brierly because this is how Marlow describes him. Brierly, we are told, "had never in his life made a mistake, never had an accident, never a mishap, never a check in his steady rise, and he seemed one of those lucky fellows who know nothing of indecision, much less of self-mistrust."[54] He was the sailor's sailor, the captain's captain. "At thirty-two he had one of the best commands going in the Eastern trade—and, what's more, he thought a lot of what he had."[55] Not that Brierly was puffed up beyond his measure, inflated. His high estimation of himself was based upon genuine accomplishments and proven merits. Chatting with him during interludes in the trial, even Marlow, a respected ship's captain himself, cannot help but to feel "lesser than." This was simply the effect that Brierly had. As Marlow puts it, even "had you been the Emperor of East and West you could not have ignored your inferiority in his presence ..."[56] And yet, as exasperating as this was, when Marlow reflected that he had this inferiority in common with all the rest of humanity, "[he] found that he could bear [his] share of [Brierly's] good-natured and contemptuous pity for the sake of something indefinite and attractive in the man."[57]

Captain Brierly, clearly, is the embodiment of the ideal sailor. Not only are Duty and Professionalism handsomely enshrined in his person; what Marlow had earlier referred to as the "sovereign power enthroned in a fixed standard of conduct" is marvellously exemplified by him as well. But then, reading on, we soon learn that he was just as much a casualty of the rupture in the soul as were the *Patna* and Jim! I refer to the fact that immediately upon concluding his description of Captain Brierly's sterling qualities, Marlow springs on us the information that *shortly after the inquest Brierly committed suicide!* It is shocking news, as shocking as the hull-breaching collision of the *Patna*, as shocking as the shipmate Jim's conduct-breaching dereliction of his duty as a sailor, and yet it may be regarded as an analogy for the same thing, i.e., for the aforementioned rupture in the soul. In Captain Brierly's suicide is represented "the soul's" relentless facing up to the fact that the times of the truths he had embodied are over![58]

But there is another side to this as well, a subjective side. A character in a modernist novel, Captain Brierly is also portrayed in terms of the personal side of the psychological difference.[59] Speculating about the reason that he stepped off his ship to make a grave for himself in the sea, Marlow opines that while seeming to be bored by Jim's case "he was probably holding silent inquiry into his own case."[60] Some trifle on Brierly's conscience, something known only to himself alone, so contradicted his image of himself that it somehow got the better of him. It must have been something like that, offers Marlow. But when we listen in to the conversation the two captains actually have about Jim's case, another picture emerges. Whether Brierly, the man, had some skeleton in his closet or not (and we should remember that he is not a man with such and such a psychology,[61] but a character in a novel, a personification), what brings about his demise in Marlow's and the reader's eyes is his difference-less identification with the objective demise of the ideal he represents. When Marlow points out Jim's moral fiber and courage, as exemplified by his staying in port to face the consequences of his dishonourable conduct, Brierly will have nothing of it. Better that Jim would hasten away like the others than by sticking around for the inquest cause the profession's dirty laundry to be aired publicly. In Brierley's view the shame of the matter at hand is greater than this one man, Jim. Indeed, it is downright "abominable."[62] Countering this extreme reaction, Marlow coldly declares that the cowardice of Jim and the three others that abandoned ship was no matter of great importance. But Brierly will not abide this narrowing of the focus to these particular individuals, as if the cowardice they displayed were only a mishap for them, only their problem. "'And you call yourself a seaman, I suppose,' [Brierly] pronounced angrily." Back and forth they went about it until, making "a gesture with his big arm that seemed to deprive [Marlow] of [his] individuality, [and] to push [him] away into the crowd," Brierly witheringly declared, "The worst of it … is that all you fellows have no sense of dignity; you don't think enough of what you are supposed to be."[63]

TARRYING WITH THE NEGATIVE
TRANSFORMING THE WILL

The significance of Captain Brierly's suicide resides in the fact that it brings out the truth of Jim's failure as a seaman even as Jim's failure as a seaman brings out the demise of the ideal which the impeccable Brierly had exemplified and existed as. Both characters equally are the expression of the rupture in the soul occurring in their times. The only difference between them in this regard is that Jim maintains himself in the face of the death that the ideal-exemplifying Brierly succumbs to when he steps into the sea shortly after the inquest. Now, of course, in speaking as I just have of the disgraced Jim maintaining himself in the face of death, I allude to Hegel's famous lines about "tarrying with the negative." In Hegel's view, the life of the spirit is such that it "wins its truth only when, in utter dismemberment, it finds itself." Continuing he states: "It is this power, not as something positive, which closes its eyes to the negative as when we say of something that it is nothing or is false, and then having done with it, turn away and pass on to something else; on the contrary, spirit is this power only by looking the negative in the face, and tarrying with it. This tarrying with the negative is the magical power that converts it into being."[64] Our novel, let it be grasped, reflects this same process of determinate negation via the figures of Captain Brierly and Jim. Within itself that traditional truth of the soul that in the novel is variously referred to as duty, dignity of office, the ideal of a fixed standard of conduct, and by still other expressions dirempts itself to become Brierly, on the one hand, and Jim, on the other. And it is in this way, as we shall see, that Duty's meaning is transformed from having the form of an abstract imperative (in the manner, say, of a commandment issued from on high) to having the form of a humble this-worldly imperative of integrity which is both more subtle and comprehensive than its idealized precursor due to the integration of what at first had seemed an offense against it.[65]

Looking into this subject matter more closely, we see on the Captain Brierly side of the rupture in the soul that is expressed in the difference between him and Jim what Jung would later call a "conservative adherence to the earlier attitude."[66] Reiterating the abstract meaning of the duty that he stands for, Brierly bitterly rues the disgrace that the inquiry into the *Patna* case is allowing to be put on display. It is only proper, he maintains, that "professional decency" be preserved, and with this end in mind he irritably suggests that Marlow and he pool their money together to send Jim away before he brings even more embarrassment upon their profession by appearing in court! But all this rings hollow for Marlow.[67] Even if Jim is only the first immediacy of an unknown successor value that has yet to be fleshed out, he already stands for something better than the sham that Brierly has shown his duty-for-duty's-sake stance to be through his dishonest idea of instituting a cover-up on its behalf. Indeed, as Marlow states after hearing Brierly out, it was only then that "I became positive in my mind that the inquiry was a severe punishment for … Jim, and that his facing it—practically of his own free will—was a redeeming feature in his abominable case."[68]

The question arises. Was the tarrying with the negative that Jim's facing the inquest "practically of his own free will" exemplifies already evident on the deck of the *Patna* when, in the midst of the crisis, he failed in his duty? Or to ask the same question in another way, was the failure of Jim's will as a seaman already the soul's own doing, i.e., the productive expression of its self-negation?[69]

We already know from Marlow that in those days duty was so drilled into young sailors that by the time they were fully credentialed seaman it was "the component part of every waking thought, … [and] present in every dream of their young sleep!"[70] But when the fully credentialed Jim sees the breach in the *Patna's* hull he suffers a Hamlet-like moment of indecision and doubt. Disaster, he senses, is imminent, the ship but moments from sinking. And as if this were not already enough to beggar the hero within him, he is stymied as well by his knowledge that there are too few lifeboats to even begin to accommodate the large number of passengers. From this, we may surmise, it was his very fate to fail.

Now when I say, "fate to fail," I again have in mind the aforementioned rent in the times of which Jim was the discombobulated heir. It is when the times are "out of joint"[71] that that first born of the dead, the anti-hero, is born.[72] Whereas previously, that is, before such a wayward protagonist blunders to the front, every task and challenge had been straightforwardly a matter of "going up and over," as it were, in the disjunctive times that followed it was a matter, rather, of "going under and across."[73] And so it was with Hamlet and Jim. Just as our disgraced chief ship's mate's Shakespearean forbearer did not avenge his father's murder (when doing so would have been in keeping with the tradition), so in his time's version of this disjunctive moment Jim did not abide by and fulfil his professional duty. This, however (or so I am arguing here), cannot be attributed to a personal failing, for the possibility of the personal in this sense, and along with this, of a truly free will (such as Jim subsequently displayed by sticking around to testify at the inquest), only became a possibility in the first place as the *result* of the objectively occurring rupture in the soul that this scene in the story depicts.[74] For Duty in the traditional sense was already ghostly by Jim's time, as it was already becoming in a certain respect in the time of Shakespeare's *Hamlet*. When Marlow, as we already discussed, made reference to duty, it was to its having given way to and become that "most obstinate *ghost* of man's creation, ... the doubt of the sovereign power enthroned in a fixed standard of conduct."[75] And so it is that the jumping to his duty that the flummoxed Jim finally manages to execute has the disgraceful form of his obeying the ill-addressed command of his dishonourable skipper to leap into the lifeboat in desertion of his duty.

It happened like this. Mistaking his shape in the darkness for that of another colleague they wished to save, the Captain, Chief

Engineer, and another officer had repeatedly yelled up from the life-boat, "Jump, George! We'll catch you! Jump!"[76] As Jim explains later to Marlow, although he had by that point been resigned to dying, in the next instant the past tense had overtaken him inasmuch as he had then to realize that *he had already jumped!* Experientially, it was as if that jump had not been his action at all, but a matter of being pulled, as by a boat-hook, by the commands he had heard.[77] But, of course, it *was* his action. As he put it himself, "I had jumped." Which is why immediately upon finding himself in the lifeboat, his shame was so immense. "I wished I could die … There was no going back. It was as if I had jumped into a well—into an everlasting deep hole …"[78] The point to be grasped, complementary to our interest here, which is to explore the formal and final (i.e., soulful) causes of Jim's abandoning ship, is that his failure's efficient cause is described as having had fluke character. As Conrad's prose makes clear, Jim's honour-wrecking leap from the deck of the *Patna* into the lifeboat was like a Freudian slip, except for the fact that psychically it was even more underdetermined than that.

After this digression, let us return to the topic of what truly makes for the dishonourable conduct which the story of Jim reflects. Although we can hardly grasp anymore what the concepts of duty and honour meant during those earlier times when "man had his being and essence in the Universal [such that] *in essential regards* he did not live *his own* life [but] '*was lived*' by the customs and ritual necessities of his culture…,"[79] some reflection upon this question might be of interest to us in our work with the later-day Jims we meet with in our practices and in ourselves.

Were Jim not a character in a novel, but an actual person of those times, we might direct him to the great American psychologist of that period for insight concerning the failure of his will to duty. In the chapter on "The Will" in his *Principles of Psychology*, William James defines the will as the seamless unity of thought and action, as when, for example, we just like that raise our arm at will or move our mouths at the same moment as we think of having a nice meal.[80]

Lapses of the will, failures of action or reaction, on the other hand, he attributes to a disunity of motive ideas.[81] When a person, for example, finds himself subject to a variety of different imperative thoughts and perspectives—and surely what we have been calling "the splitting of the world" and "the rupture in the soul" are the extreme version of these!—he may be halted by his inability to serve these various masters at the same time.[82] But Jim is not a person in life, he is a character in a novel. As such, he is the artistically-rendered *product* of the split in the world or rupture in the soul which he appears to be obstructed by, the personification of the idea through which the soul's finding into its own expresses its truth at the threshold of a new epoch. There is not first a Jim who in addition to being an existing person then fails in his duty. On the contrary, it is only through this failure as a quality of the times that the novel reflects that he becomes Jim in the first place. Waxing as Brierly wanes, Jim is an idea. Which may be why he "always seemed symbolic"[83] to Marlow, who at one point even found it "difficult to believe in Jim's existence."[84] Although presented as a failing young man, Jim is "the soul's" first inkling of the new conception through which it can exert its will once more. "In action as in reasoning," writes James, "the great thing is the quest for the right conception."[85] Locking his fingers together and pulling them apart again as he talks to Marlow,[86] the disgraced Jim, I submit, is a faltering approximation of the right conception. Appearing at a time when the traditional sense of duty was in decline, his character pioneers the successor form of duty—let us call it the duty attendant upon having become self—in the admirable way in which he embraced his fate and makes the most of it.

THE LORDSHIP OF SUBLATED FAILURE

We have yet to inquire into how Jim, after being stripped of his credentials as a seaman, subsequently came to be honoured with the title Lord Jim. Without going into the many details of the rich and varied plot, it will suffice for our purposes to merely state that after holding and departing from many waterside jobs—in such places as Bombay, Calcutta, Rangoon, Penang, Bangkok, and Batavia—Jim finally took up a post in the extremely remote Malay island kingdom of Patusan. So remote was this kingdom that it was practically unknown to white men, which also meant for Jim that his flight from being recognized as the disgraced sailor of the *Patna* fiasco had reached its nadir and turning point. Viewed in one way, Jim's having come to live in this remote kingdom, so far from his own kind, showed that the alienation consequent upon his dishonourable leap into the lifeboat had become absolute. But viewed from within this condition, from within the very heart of its darkness (if I may put it this way with another of Conrad's novels in mind[87]), it was at the same time the opposite of this, what in dialectics of sublation is called the restored position.[88]

It happened like this: when Jim arrived among the Malay natives of Patusan he found that the society there was riven by strife on several fronts. Displaying martial ingenuity, strategic know-how, and a courageous fighting spirit Jim at once threw himself into the cause of helping the long-reigning and rightful kingdom to prevail over its enemies. Whereas previously he had failed in his duty when he served on the *Patna*, he brilliantly distinguished himself in this new setting. Indeed, so impressed were the natives by their white saviour that they thenceforth treated him with reverent respect. Tuan Jim, Lord Jim, they called him. And so it was that for many years he served as the most trusted advisor of the people and their aged chieftain-king,[89] his wise counsel and selfless dedication earning him the esteem of a demi-god.

Now surely, as analysts we are again and again in our practices as struck with wonder as was our literary forbearer, Captain Marlow, when he learned of Jim's life amongst the Malay and when he visited with him there. Why, sometimes it is even as if the sweep of this whole novel were collapsed into a single analytic hour, occasionally, even, into the very first hour. The patient lays out his difficulties. He tells us of some misstep he regrets, or some dilemma in which he is stuck. However different the details may be in each individual case, this moment of odious disclosures may be likened to that one in which, after confessing his dishonourable conduct, Jim looks up to Marlow with a "piteous stare," even as Marlow seeing him standing there so "dumbfounded and hurt, ... [is] oppressed by a sad sense of resigned wisdom, mingled with the amused and profound pity of an old man helpless before a childish disaster."[90] But then on the heels of this a dream may be presented in which, like the Jim who became Lord Jim in a remote Malay kingdom, the patient's dream-I finds itself in a weird, uncanny setting, tasked with a strange, and yet, defining adventure![91]

"Two things fill the mind with ever new and increasing admiration and awe, the more often and steadily we reflect upon them," writes Kant: "the starry heavens above me and the moral law within me. I do not seek or conjecture either of them as if they were veiled obscurities or extravagances beyond the horizon of my vision; I see them before me and connect them immediately with the consciousness of my existence."[92] I think of these lines from that great Enlightenment philosopher whenever I come upon such scenes of moral infinitude and life-task universality as we are discussing here, be these in the dreams of my patients or in the Patusan sequence of Conrad's novel. In both cases what externally or from an ego point of view is a piteous calamity, a cause for fret and care (i.e., the aforementioned "presenting problem"), is inwardly or from the point of view of the self presented, *sub specie aeternitatis*, as a larger, perhaps even magnificent, moral and ethical soul-making challenge. And here, apropos of this comment, I am reminded as well of a passage from a letter Jung wrote which addresses the topic of psychological transformation.

> What I call transformation is at bottom a question of fate. Although we may wish to keep within our limits, or to overstep them, it is never done by wishing but only by happening. Only when it happens to us that we overstep our

limits can we be sure that we have overstepped them and that it had to be so. In the end there is no legitimate having-to-go-beyond-ourselves. Hence I would not recommend anybody to wish to go beyond himself. Moreover this expression is false; we cannot go beyond ourselves but only deeper into ourselves, and this self is not identical with the ego *because in this self we appear wondrously strange to ourselves.*"[93]

It is the last phrase of this quotation that I want especially to emphasize. Regardless of whether Jim's, our patients', or our own aspirations have been governed by a wish to keep within our own limits or to overstep them, what actually comes to pass, what actually happens, be it for weal or for woe, comes subsequently to be reflected as our "*appear[ing] wondrously strange to ourselves.*"[94] And how wondrously strange, indeed, was Jim in the jungle kingdom of Patusan,[95] living the ethical life of a hallowed saviour figure amongst the Malay natives, his fiercely loving, protective, and devoted wife, the Eurasian girl, Jewel, by his side.[96] A far cry, this, from the prospect which Marlow worried about after the inquest that the demoralized Jim would end up a degenerate alcoholic![97]

PSYCHOLOGY, OR: THE RESTORATION OF DUTY REDEFINED

After this very brief account of how Jim endeavored to become the master of his fate, let us return to our theme of the rise of psychology from out of the dereliction of duty.

It would certainly be plausible, further to what was discussed in the previous section, to fix our focus upon how Jim as an individual person runs into various difficulties and tarries with these as the mediators of that self-negating/self-sublating dialectic of life which Jung called the individuation process. Viewed in this light, his story well-illustrates Jung's insight that "If a man is contradicted by himself and … knows that he contradicts himself, he is individuated."[98] But our interest is less in the individuation process of a particular person than in that moment in what has been called "the individuation of mankind"[99] in which the possibility of such a character as Jim, be it in literature or in life, became possible in the first place. Just as psychology arose in the wake of the religion and metaphysics that preceded it,[100] so our novel's protagonist, Jim, as well as his double in our patients and in ourselves, *was the result*, not merely of his own dereliction of duty, but of the real negation and objective demise of the traditional symbolic forms of the soul that had been the ground of such duteous conduct.

Now with this important insight we come to the heart of what clinical psychoanalysis can learn from its literary other. There is a difference to be discerned—our school of psychology calls it a "psychological difference"[101]—between taking the Jim character literally as an empirical person with such and such a temperament and upbringing, and taking him figuratively and post-symbolically (!) as the anti-heroic poster-boy of the soul's own demise. Though we are all, as St. Augustine put it, "born between faeces and urine," and thus *psychically* subject to the anxieties and slip-ups that are occasioned by what Freud would later describe as infantile sexuality and the Oedipus complex, logically, *psychologically*, we are also born, insofar as the universality of the human spirit is concerned, from out of the aforementioned rupture in the soul, wherein the world, as it were, has pulled out from under the tradition that had provided for every need and action. Depicted in our novel as Jim's dishonourable leap from the *Patna*, our birth from this very different gash corresponds to that moment in the history of the soul that Giegerich has thematized under the title "The End of Meaning and the Birth of Man."[102]

Now when I speak of Jim as being *the result* of the objective going under of the soul's symbolic forms during a time when their correspondence with the world had been logically breached by the enormous changes that the Enlightenment period and the Industrial Age brought, I am immediately put in mind of another famous passage from Hegel, this one having to do with his concept of sublation. "*To sublate* and *being sublated* (the *idealized*)," writes Hegel,

> constitute one of the most important concepts of philosophy. It is a fundamental determination that repeatedly occurs everywhere in it, the meaning of which must be grasped with precision and especially distinguished from *nothing*.—What is sublated does not thereby turn into nothing. Nothing is *immediate*; something sublated is on the contrary something mediated; it is something non-existent but as a result that has proceeded from a being; it still *has in itself*, therefore, the *determinateness from which it derives*.[103]

In keeping with the insight of this passage we can say the same of Jim. Far from being reduced to nothing by his failure to do his duty, Jim is the *sublated result* of the duties, ideals, and soul-truths that had become obsolete during the times that his story reflects. In the novel, this is conveyed by means of the contrast between him and the other officers who also abandoned ship. For example, upon being dishonourably released from the soul by his self-interested and deplorable conduct, the despicable skipper of the *Patna* simply escapes, without further ado, into the undialectical, anything-goes freedom of a mere rogue. Jim's emancipation, by contrast, has an entirely different character. Even after being stripped of his credentials he continues to have, or better, to be the personification of "the determinateness from which [these had] derive[d]."[104] It is a matter, as we said before, of "tarrying with the negative." Or drawing upon yet another Hegelian figure, a matter of "Substance [i.e., Duty] show[ing] itself to be essentially Subject [e.g., Jim]."[105] In the passion and turmoil of Jim's subsequent coming to terms with his fate, Duty is not simply broken with, but determinately negated, kenotically repurposed.[106] From being defined as one's living up to that role within the divine order of things that Tradition has assigned, it navigates a form-change to become, *post mortem dei*, the imperative of becoming self in the down-to-earth sense of finding into one's own integrity, one's own truth.[107] And so it is that the story of Jim's disgrace as a sailor is the story of the movement from "the soul" in the traditional sense of its meaning to psychology as its logically negative successor.[108]

JIM'S DEATH

I want to bring these reflections to a close by briefly touching upon the tragic confluence of character and circumstance within which Jim met his final end. In the last pages of the novel, the story of Jim's magnificent career amongst the Malay gives way in a treacherous debacle involving a blood-thirsty pirate, known as Gentleman Brown, who easily manages to take advantage of Jim's idealistic principles and gentlemanly standard of conduct. A deserter turned buccaneer, Brown is described as holding a high rank amongst the most notorious scoundrels of that period owing to "the arrogant temper of his misdeeds and [his] vehement scorn for mankind at large and for his victims in particular."[109] Chancing upon the remote island village of Patusan, he and his crew immediately desire to capture it for themselves, to loot and destroy it, even as, in accordance with the office he has so brilliantly held up until this point, Jim's reciprocal task is to protect the people of Patusan from the dire threat this poses to their lives and property. And so it is that the intrepid Jim sets out to have a parley with Brown.

The crucial scene comes shortly before the violent turmoil that unfolds from it afterwards. At "the very spot where Jim [had taken] the second desperate leap of his life—the leap that landed him into the life of Patusan, into the trust, the love, the confidence of the people,"[110] he and Brown come face to face on opposite sides of a creek. Will Jim prove worthy of his lordship in this lurch come around again? Will he be up to this latest version of the uncanny test his life has been about? The situation is clear enough. Jim knows Brown to be an evil-intentioned and nefarious character. Despite this, however, his judgement and resolution are compromised by his regarding Brown as if he and the rest of his crew were "the emissaries with whom the world [Jim] had renounced was pursuing him in retreat—white men from 'out there' where he did not think himself good enough to live."[111] It is amazing the grip that this shame-complex (or of what we would regard as such if he were a person) still has upon Jim. Despite all that he has made of himself in Patusan, and the trust he has won there, Jim continues to think himself unworthy, even before these criminals! From this we may surmise that he still takes his dereliction of duty subjectively, personally, and does not realize that the going under of this traditional ideal was something objective and that the character ascribed to him in the novel is more the result of this than its cause.[112]

No wonder, then, the dialectic of his having to meet his *bête noir* in Captain Brown. Jim has tried to climb out of his going under, rather than submitting to the chaotic element that belongs to his time's sublation. I allude with this wording to what are perhaps the most often quoted lines of the novel:

> A man that is born falls into a dream like a man who falls into the sea. If he tries to climb out into the air as inexperienced people endeavour to do, he drowns—*nicht wahr?* .... No! I tell you! The way is to the destructive element submit yourself, and with the exertions of your hands and feet in the water make the deep, deep sea keep you up.[113]

It is because Jim tries to climb out of *his* Disgrace and *his* Dishonour, and to cleave once more to the values he believed *himself* to have failed, that the chaotic element must take the form of the violent and terrible Gentleman Brown.[114]

And this is not all. There is yet another reason for this final episode. Jim, it is explicitly stated in the novel, is a romantic.[115] As such, he personifies the Romantic era's Beautiful Soul-like[116] resistance with respect to the decline of the traditional soul values that the Enlightenment and the Industrial Revolution had wrought. Little wonder, then, that the terrible Captain Brown "sails into Jim's history,"[117] there to give the lie to the repristination project that Jim personifies of indulging in the values and truths of a bygone time. Just as much later Jung, indulging in his own version of such anachronistic soulfulness, once asked himself, on the very heels of realizing that we no longer have or live in myth, "then what is your myth—the myth in which you do live?,"[118] so Jim naively persists in the duty, decorum, and ideals he believed himself earlier to have failed, only to be taken in by Brown as by the aforementioned emissary of the world he had departed from. As Marlow puts it in his account of this exchange, "When [Brown] asked Jim, with a sort of brusque despairing frankness, whether he himself—straight now—didn't understand that when 'it came to saving one's life in the dark, one didn't care who else went—three, thirty, three hundred people'—it was as if a demon had been whispering advice in his ear." Mortified by his interlocutor's statement, Jim lowered his gaze to the ground. Brown, however, did not let up, but rather put the knife more deeply in by asking "whether [Jim] had nothing fishy in his life to remember ..."[119] And when these words, so evocative for Jim of the *Patna* affair, were spoken "there ran through the rough talk a vein of subtle reference to their common blood, an assumption of common experience; a sickening suggestion of common guilt, of secret knowledge that was like a bond of their minds and of their hearts."[120]

But Brown was a shadow that Jim could not integrate, at least not in any other way than by the dialectic of the demise which his figure mediated.[121] Romantic to the end, Jim continued to play the high-minded and honourable gentleman, which meant taking the decision to let Brown go in peace, rather than defeating him decisively when he had the upper hand. It was a terrible misjudgement. After making a show of keeping to their agreement, the treacherous Brown doubled back and attacked the village, killing the King's son and many more besides.[122] With this turn of events, Jim's otherwise laudable effort to live down his past disgrace achieved its tragic end. As Marlow summing up Jim's understanding of the situation put it, "He had retreated from one world, for a small matter of an impulsive jump, and now the other, the work of his own hands, had fallen in ruins upon his head."[123] Jim being Jim, however, there was at this point only one course of action to be followed. Just as before, when after the *Patna* fiasco he had stayed to appear at the inquest (and a comparison may also be drawn to Captain Brierly's resolutely stepping into the sea), he followed up this failure by solemnly appearing before the tribal king, who he had until this point so loyally and sagely served, to accept death by his anguished bullet.

The shot was a fatal one. Immediately upon its being fired, the crowd rushed forward to the side of their dying white lord, who with the last of his strength "sent ... at all those faces a proud and unflinching glance."[124] And so it was, as his now bereaved friend, Marlow, bitterly put it, that Jim went on "to celebrate his pitiless wedding with a shadowy ideal of conduct."[125] But for this 19th Century European figure, the time of kings and other such regents of the soul was over, which is why he had had quixotically to go into the jungle to still find the likes of one to serve. In the final analysis, however, this was untenable. There was no escaping the objectively prevailing dereliction of duty from which the age of psychology emerged, not even for that last romantic, our proto-patient, the disgraced ship's officer, Jim.

Extensive Endnotes in Lieu of a Seminar

[1] *Lord Jim*, pp. 111-112.

[2] So literary were Freud's clinical papers that on one occasion, this was in the "Prefatory Remarks" to his paper on Dora, he issued an ambivalent rebuke to the "many physicians who (revolting though it may seem) choose to read a case history of this kind not as a contribution to the psycho-pathology of neuroses, but as a *roman à clef* designed for their private delectation." Sigmund Freud, "Fragment of an analysis of a case of hysteria," in *Collected Papers*, Alix & James Strachey, trans., London: The Hogarth Press & The Institute of Psycho-Analysis, vol. III, p.15. My approach in this paper is precisely the opposite of Freud's—to read a literary work as if it were a contribution to clinical psychoanalysis, but without reducing it to the presuppositions or positivized findings of the latter.

[3] Reference to "soul" is indispensable for what I am attempting to show in this essay, since it is the precursor term for what later became psychology. While being roughly equivalent to "consciousness" and "mindedness," it enriches these with historical associations from the times of ritual and myth, religion and metaphysics. Differently than in the past that the term remembers, however, it is not to be conceived of by us in ontological terms as an existing substance. Soul is not a thing. Logically negative, it rather has thought character. Which is why there is a convention in psychology as the discipline of interiority to place quotation marks around the word, or to always read and write it as if it were in quotation marks. For more on this topic see Wolfgang Giegerich, *What Is Soul?*, New Orleans: Spring Journal Books, 2012, pp. 21-25, 291.

[4] For the seminal contribution on this topic see Wolfgang Giegerich, *The Soul's Logical Life: Towards a Rigorous Notion of Psychology*, Frankfurt am Main: Peter Lang, 1998.

[5] Sonu Shamdasani, "A Woman called Frank," *Spring 50: A Journal of Archetype and Culture*, 1990, p. 40.

[6] *Lord Jim*, pp. 44, 74, 100, 112, 121, 208, 283, 287, 310, 351.

---

[7] *Lord Jim*, p. 67, my emphasis.

[8] Jung, *CW* 8 § 396; *CW* 10 § 766; *CW* 14 § 45, 700.

[9] *Lord Jim*, p. 67.

[10] G.W. F. Hegel, *The Philosophy of Right*, T. M. Knox, trans., Oxford: Oxford University Press, 1967, p. 13.

[11] *Lord Jim*, p. 84.
[12] *Lord Jim*, p. 84.
[13] *Lord Jim*, p. 84.
[14] *Lord Jim*, p. 84.

[15] As if "taking professional opinion on the case"(p. 152), Marlow repeatedly discusses Jim with friends and acquaintances. It is important for what we are attempting here that our own theories and opinions about Jim be given no more status than is given to the ones that are presented by the characters in the novel. Steeped though I am in psychology as the discipline of interiority, I am imposing this restriction upon my use of its theory of neurosis in these pages. No doubt, a strong reading along those lines is possible. Nineteenth century Jim clinging to soul truths that are no longer true nicely exemplifies Giegerich's account of neurosis as a malady of the soul that became possible in that century. But our interest is in "the return from otherness" (Hegel) that our psychological approach(es) may glean from Conrad's novel. This, I submit, has largely do to with the intentional ambivalence that Conrad as author, and Marlow as narrator, are able to sustain toward "the mystery of [Jim's] attitude." Just as Freud talked of listening with "evenly-suspended attention," Jung of "not knowing beforehand," and Bion of starting each session "without memory or desire," so we can glean something of value for our analytic attitude from what literary critics have called "Conradian ambivalence." Giving a hint about this, I would simply say at this point that from Conrad and Marlow we can learn something about the discernment of when in therapy a final-synthetic (i.e., soul-making) approach should be taken and when the approach should be more reductively-analytical and cauterizing. About this distinction see Jung, *CW* 7 § 121-140 and Giegerich, *What is Soul?*, pp. 317-335.

[16] See the discussion of Gadamer's principle of *applicatio* in Giegerich, "The

Provenance of C.G. Jung's Psychological Findings," *CEP*, vol. I, p. 135.

[17] *Lord Jim*, p. 72.
[18] *Lord Jim*, p. 72, Conrad's ellipsis.
[19] *Lord Jim*, p. 72-73.

[20] Jung, *CW* 16 § 534.

[21] In his "Author's Note," at the front of the novel, Conrad writes of his encounter with what might be called "the Jim in us all": "One morning in the commonplace surroundings of an Eastern roadstead, I saw his form pass by—appealing—significant—under a cloud [= in trouble, disfavour, or disgrace]—perfectly silent. Which is as it should be. It was for me, with all the sympathy of which I was capable, to seek fit words for his meaning. He was 'one of us.'" *Lord Jim*, p. 44.

[22] *Lord Jim*, p. 75.
[23] *Lord Jim*, p. 75.
[24] *Lord Jim*, p. 80.

[25] Sigmund Freud, "Some Character Types met with in Psycho-Analytic Work," section II, "Those Wrecked by Success," *Collected Papers*, London: The Hogarth Press & The Institute of Psycho-Analysis, 1950, vol. IV, pp. 323-341.

[26] It is the *impeccable,* the *honourable* Captain Marlow who finds his other in Jim. Transposing this literary idea into the terms of my claim that their relationship anticipates that of the analyst and patient, we can say that Marlow apperceived Jim via an non-neurotic, psychologically acute, self-othering positive countertransference. In Jungian parlance, this would be to say that Jim is like the lapis *in via ejectus/exilis* and is valued—or rather, re-valued—by Marlow as such (see Jung, *CW* 5 § 276). A passage deleted by Conrad from his final version of the novel, but arguably still present within it (in a contained, not acted-out, i.e., deleted manner!), is pertinent in this connection. Sitting at Jim's inquest, Marlow comments about the other people in attendance: " … they seemed to me strange, foreign, *as if* belonging to some other order of beings I had no connection with. It was only when my eyes turned towards Jim that I had a sense of not being alone of my kind, as if we two had wandered in from some distant regions, from a different world. I turned to him for fellowship. He alone seemed to look natural." Cited in Ian Watt, *Conrad in the Nineteenth Century*, Berkeley/Los

Angeles: University of California Press, 1979, p. 316.

[27] In this connection, I am put in mind of how in Kafka's novel, *The Trial*, the protagonist Josef K is similarly concerned that if he were to write an exculpatory treatise it would have to be very lengthy since "ignorance of the actual charges … would make it necessary to survey and describe [his] whole life from every conceivable angle, [and] to recall to mind the very smallest actions and events." Franz Kafka, *The Trial*, Douglas Scoot & Chris Waller, trans., London: Pan Books, 1977, p. 149.

[28] For a discussion of the topic of psychology as *ersatz* for soul see Giegerich, *What is Soul?*, pp. 140-146.

[29] Duty must be capitalized in this context to indicate its status as a value or truth of the soul. Such an indication is indispensable for a psychology that understands itself as having emerged as the sublation of the metaphysics that preceded it. Bachelard, with a similar sensibility to mine here, writes of a "psychology of capital letters." Gaston Bachelard, *The Poetics of Reverie: Childhood, Language, and the Cosmos*, trans. D. Russell, Boston: Beacon paperback, 1971, p. 173.

[30] *Lord Jim*, p. 97.

[31] I said it is difficult for a patient to see his symptom as the first immediacy of his own cure. Conrad's prose, however, is capable of this duplex vision. While Jim's violent touchiness with respect to being called a coward is clearly presented as a narcissistic wound or complex, it takes on a positive, prospective meaning after his trial in the form of a stance expressive of his resolve thenceforth to stand up for himself and make the most of his life. After his trial, the decertified Jim says to Marlow, "Something's paid of—not much. I wonder what's to come" (p. 174). Along the same lines, it may be added that Jim's wondering "what's to come" suggests that his going to ever more distant outposts has also a prospective meaning. In keeping with this possibility, Marlow states, "I could never make up my mind about … whether his line of conduct [i.e., his leaving one job for the next when his past caught up with him] amounted to shirking his ghost or to facing him out" (*Lord Jim*, p. 187).

[32] Viewed as an actual person, Jim's penchant for taking flight each time his story catches up with him amounts to his evading any further facing up to his truth. At the same time, however, it is in this way, via these iterations,

that his character as a literary figure mediates the advent of the new truth that has been given with the form change of his times. "[A] lost youngster, one in a million … ," Jim, we are told, is at the same time "an individual in the forefront of his kind." Even as he dodges his truth, it is "as if the obscure truth involved [in his case] were momentous enough to affect mankind's conception of itself …" See the epigraph at the top of this essay for a fuller citation of this passage.

[33] Jung, *CW* 5 § 329.

[34] Giegerich, "Psychology as the Study of the Soul's Logical Life," *CEP*, vol. IV, pp. 325-350.

[35] Jung, *CW* 9, I § 400, trans. modified.

[36] For an in-depth discussion of the speculative significance of a reader's underlining of sentences, see my "Interiorizing an Underlined Sentence into Itself: Some Reflection's on Being '*Only* That!'" In Jennifer Sandoval and John Knapp, eds, *Psychology as the Discipline of Interiority: "The Psychological Difference" in the work of Wolfgang Giegerich*, London & New York: Routledge, 2017, pp. 66-81.

[37] 24 November 1953, in C. G. Jung, *Letters*, 2 vols. Gerhard Adler, ed., Bollingen Series XCV: 2, Princeton: Princeton University Press, 1975, vol. 2, p. 138. Jung adds that "Christ is still the valid symbol. Only God himself can 'invalidate' him through the Paraclete." For other references to the metaphysical split in Christianity and in God's wholeness see Jung's *Memories, Dreams, Reflections*, A. Jaffé, ed., R. & C. Winston, trans., New York: Vintage Books, 1965, p. 333

[38] For a thoroughgoing discussion of this topic see Wolfgang Giegerich, *Neurosis: The Logic of a Metaphysical Illness*, New Orleans: Spring Journal Books, 2013, pp. 83-101.

[39] I allude with this wording to Hegel's famous Speculative Remark: "What is sublated is not thereby reduced to nothing. Nothing is *immediate*; what is sublated, on the other hand, is the result of *mediation*; it is a nonbeing but as a *result* which has its origin in a being. It still has, therefore, *in itself* the *determinateness from which it originates*." G. W. F. Hegel, *Hegel's Science of Logic*, A.V. Miller, trans., New York: Humanity Books, 1999, p. 107.

[40] *Lord Jim*, p. 132.

[41] It is important to recognize the difference, in this regard, between Jim and the other officers who abandoned the *Patna*. Human nature being what it is, their kind has always been possible, which is why Marlow is not interested in them, but only in Jim, whose determinately-negated uprightness is a compelling matter of interest.

[42] In the plot of two of Conrad's earlier novels, *Almayer's Folly* and *An Outcast of the Islands*, the fortune of a big-hearted and prosperous captain in the merchant marine, Captain Tom Lingard, is seriously lessened, if not altogether ruined, through the betrayal of younger men he had taken under his wing and given careers to in his businesses. There are grounds for seeing through these treacherous and seemingly personalistic plots to the rupture in the soul that became manifest in the transition from sail to steam. As one literary biographer puts it, "In the reality from which Conrad was working [the fortunes of William Lingard, the real-life model for the Captain of the same last name in Conrad's prose,] … did indeed decline, not because he was betrayed but because the replacement of sail navigation by steam opened up an area which had formerly been exclusively his and made it available to all comers. There is thus a kind of parallelism between the fate of William Lingard and the fate of Conrad himself in the latter part of his career as a sailor: both were unable to prosper in the age of steam." John Batchelor, *The Life of Joseph Conrad*, Oxford: Blackwell Publisher, 1994, p. 54.

[43] *Lord Jim*, p. 54.

[44] Fyodor Dostoevsky, *The Brothers Karamazov*, Andrew R. MacAndrew, trans., New York: Bantam Books, 1970, Part Four, Book XI, Chapter 4.

[45] *Lord Jim*, p. 65. It is pertinent to cite here as well a passage in which Conrad discusses his own dislike for steamships, and this, moreover, in a way that alludes to an associated weakening of the sense of duty. In an autobiographical novel written late in his career, he tells of his having in his youth impulsively quit a job he had had as a seaman on a steamship. Referring to this as "almost a desertion," he goes on to explain: "For no reason on which a sensible person could put a finger I threw up my job—chucked my berth—left the ship of which the worst that could be said was that she was a steamship and therefore, perhaps, not entitled to that blind loyalty which …" Although he breaks off here, the reader is meant to fill in the ellipsis with thoughts of majestic sailing vessels. See Joseph Conrad, *The Shadow-Line*, New York: Vintage Books, 2007, p. 4. In another of his novels, *Youth*, Conrad again grapples with the topic of the transition from sail to

steam. A commercial sailing ship with a cargo of coal catches fire via (self-negating!) spontaneous combustion. Vividly described, the upshot of this is that, with its now furnace-like hold of burning coal, it resembles the steamships that are destined to supersede it. This idea of supersession or sublation is then reflected again in its coming to be towed in its peril by a coal-powered steamship. So fast is it towed by this steamer, however, that its flaming cargo is fanned to the point that a great explosion ensues. Far from being saved by the steamer, the sailing ship is destroyed by it.

[46] Giegerich, "Rupture, or: Psychology and Religion," in *CEP,* vol. I, p. 227.

[47] Since it is not known for certain what obstruction the *Patna* collided with, we might also offer another *psychological* possibility. In the chapter, "The Fish in Alchemy," of his *Aion: Researches into the Phenomenology of the Self,* Jung writes of a small fish that dwells in an ocean that is symbolized in alchemy as the "spirit of the world." Pertinent in our context is his statement: "The extremely small fish that dwells in the centre of the universal sea nevertheless has the power to stop the largest ships." *CW* 9, ii § 219. My point in citing this is not to suggest that the *Patna* hit a fish, there is no suggestion of that. Rather, I am inspired by the detail of such a fish being "extremely small." Jim, too, was small fry, "one in a million," as the novel put it in our epigraph quote. And, yet, to Marlow he seemed "an individual in the forefront of his kind," his case involving an "obscure truth ... momentous enough to affect mankind's conception of itself." Which brings me to a statement of Giegerich's, "... what at first appears as a content [or object] *of* consciousness is in truth the seed of what wants to become a radically new *form* of consciousness at large." Giegerich, "Is the Soul 'Deep?'—Entering and Following the Logical Movement of Heraclitus' 'Fragment 45'," in *CEP,* vol. VI, p. 149.

[48] *Lord Jim,* p. 64.
[49] *Lord Jim,* p. 76, italics mine.
[50] *Lord Jim,* p. 76.
[51] *Lord Jim,* p. 76.

[52] "The psychological question," writes Giegerich, "is not, cannot be, what and how the soul *is,* but how the soul is reflected in its manifestations. ... psychology is the study of the *reflection* in some mirror and not the study of *what* the mirror is the reflection *of.*" Thinking along these lines, we can in the case of Jim view descriptions of his "personality," scant as these are, as reflecting the soul of his times, and not be concerned with what "the mirror is the reflection of," i.e., with what usual psychology would see as his

personal psychodynamics. In actual psychotherapy, too, important insights may sometimes be gleaned from shifting the focus from the personality and personal psychodynamics to the play of the soul upon these registers. The cited passage is from Giegerich, "Is the Soul 'Deep?'—Entering and Following the Logical Movement of Heraclitus' 'Fragment 45'." In *CEP*, vol. VI, p. 132.

[53] *Lord Jim*, p. 85.
[54] *Lord Jim*, p. 85.
[55] *Lord Jim*, p. 85.
[56] *Lord Jim*, p. 85.
[57] *Lord Jim*, pp. 85-86.

[58] This interpretation of the Brierly figure's suicide is basically the same as Giegerich's interpretation of the death of the officer in Kafka's *In the Penal Colony*. When the time of his truth is over this officer dies in the punishment machine he had administered while at the same time the machine itself breaks up and destroys itself. Giegerich, "The Alchemy of History," in *CEP,* vol. III, p. 402.

[59] Each of the characters of the novel can be read as reflecting both sides of the psychological difference, the subjectively psychic and personalistic, on the one hand, and the objectively psychological, on the other. For a pertinent discussion of this see the section, "The Psychological Difference Within the Soul-As-Subject," in Giegerich, *What is Soul?*, pp. 298-300. "This ambiguity," writes Giegerich, "can of course lead to difficulties. It is our job in our psychological work to make it clear to ourselves which 'soul' is meant in each specific context, without, however, in our theorizing trying to split the unity of the two for the sake of unambiguity, for example by using two different names. The contradiction and equivocation must not be avoided. It is inherent in the psychological notion of soul" (p. 300). Conrad, I submit, is masterful at presenting the difference that the psychological difference distinguishes as running through each one of his characters. Jim, Brierly, and the rest are simultaneously presented as people in the world *and* personified universals.

[60] *Lord Jim*, p 86.

[61] For a discussion of the fallacy of psychology as the study of people who have such and such a psychology see Giegerich, *The Soul's Logical Life*, pp. 107-108, 117, 212.

---

⁶² *Lord Jim*, p. 92.

⁶³ *Lord Jim*, p. 92.

⁶⁴ G. W. F. Hegel, *Phenomenology of Spirit*, A. V. Miller, trans., Oxford: Oxford University Press, 1977, p. 19.

⁶⁵ It is edifying to compare the traditional attitude to Duty that prevailed in those earlier times when individuals had their identity and selfhood in the symbolic order of culturally assigned roles and occupations to the attitude of the psychology that came in the aftermath of the traditional soul's decline. In the following, Jung pays grudging tribute to the lingering remains of the former situation, which the emancipated individual must thenceforth deal with, not wholeheartedly, as the whole man, but through what Jung called the persona. "Society expects, and indeed must expect, every individual to play the part assigned to him as perfectly as possible so that a man who is a parson must not only carry out his official functions objectively, but must at all times and in all circumstances play the role of a parson in a flawless manner. Society demands this as a kind of surety; each must stand at his post, here a cobbler, there a poet. Nor is it advisable to be both, for that would be 'odd.' Such a man would be 'different' from other people, not quite reliable. In the academic world he would be a dilettante, in politics an 'unpredictable' quantity, in religion a free-thinker—in short, he would always be suspected of unreliability and incompetence, because society is persuaded that only the cobbler who is not a poet can supply workmanlike shoes. To present an unequivocal face to the world is a matter of practical importance: the average man—the only kind society knows anything about—must keep his nose to one thing in order to achieve anything worthwhile, two would be too much. Our society is undoubtedly set on such an ideal. It is therefore not surprising that everyone who wants to get on must take these expectations into account. Obviously, no one could completely submerge his individuality in these expectations; hence the construction of an artificial personality becomes an unavoidable necessity. The demands of propriety and good manners are an added inducement to assume a becoming mask. What goes on behind the mask is what is called 'private life.' This painfully familiar division of consciousness into two figures, often preposterously different, is an incisive psychological operation that is bound to have repercussions on the unconscious." (*CW* 7 § 305).

⁶⁶ Jung's statement: "The chief obstacle to new modes of psychological adaptation is conservative adherence to the earlier attitude" (*CW* 4 § 350).

⁶⁷ *Lord Jim*, p. 93

[68] *Lord Jim*, p. 93. When Marlow subsequently tells Jim of Brierly's idea of providing him runaway money he is humbled by Jim's response. "But I've got to get over this thing, and I mustn't shirk any of it or … I won't shirk any of it." "I may have jumped, but I don't run away" (p. 156).

[69] In a text I am inspired at this juncture to recall, Giegerich writes that "The deed 'plucks up the courage' and 'has the nerve' to bring itself into being. It owes its existence, as it were, to 'impertinence'" ("Killings," *CEP*, vol. III, p. 220). In this essay, I am making the same, or rather the obverse point, with respect to the apparent failure of Jim's nerve and courage. These, I submit, may likewise be constitutive of new forms of soul.

[70] *Lord Jim*, p. 75.

[71] William Shakespeare, *Hamlet*, Act 1, scene 5, line 190. For an allusion to *Hamlet* in the novel see *Lord Jim*, p. 199.

[72] Not only is Jim young, as stating the obvious one of Marlow's colleagues points out. More than that, he is, as Marlow puts it, "The youngest human being now in existence," (*Lord Jim*, p. 204), i.e., the earliest exemplar of Western man redefined by the times in which the story is set.

[73] With the second expression, "going under and across," I allude to the similar movement emphasized by Nietzsche. In "Zarathustra's Prologue," for example, we read that "what is great in man is that he is a bridge and not a goal; what can be loved in man is that he is a *going-across* and a *down-going* [*übergang und untergang*]." Friedrich Nietzsche, *Thus Spoke Zarathustra*, R. J. Hollingdale, trans., Harmondsworth, U.K: Penguin Books, 1969, p. 44.

[74] Related to Duty as a casualty of the objectively occurring rupture in the soul (we could also say, related to it as the other side of the same coin) is a doubt that is not merely subjective or personal, but a status of consciousness in modernity. For an in-depth discussion of this topic see the section "'Doubt' as the intrinsic form of truth in modernity," in Giegerich's "'Jung and Hegel' Revisited," *CEP*, vol. VI, pp. 354-364.

[75] *Lord Jim*, p. 80. Italics mine.
[76] *Lord Jim*, p. 125.
[77] *Lord Jim*, p. 134.

[78] *Lord Jim*, p. 125.

[79] Giegerich, *Neurosis: The Logic of a Metaphysical Illness*, p. 84. For a pertinent discussion of the emptying out of honour that has become especially evident since 1900, see Giegerich, "The Occidental Soul's Self-Immurement in Plato's Cave," *CEP*, vol. II, p. 258.

[80] William James, *The Briefer Course*, Gordon Allport, ed., New York: Harper & Row, 1961, p. 293.

[81] James, *The Briefer Course*, p. 293: "… *every representation of a movement awakens in some degree the actual movement which is its object; and awakens it in a maximum degree whenever it is not kept from so doing by an antagonistic representation present simultaneously to the mind*" (p. 293), italics in original.

[82] In addition to the will-confounding rupture in the soul that I am discussing in terms of "sail" and "steam," Tradition and the Industrial Revolution, we should also recall the disillusioning effect of Darwin's theories, which were also gaining wide acceptance during the time in which Conrad wrote and in which the novel is set. The change brought to the definition of Man by his theory of natural selection and the descent of man must surely be regarded as an important factor in taking the wind out of Jim's vainglorious sails. For, indeed, Jim's behaviour in the *Patna* crisis was arguably more in keeping with, more governed by, that motive theory than it was by the God-hallowing Traditional values of duty and honour that he failed. My thanks to Daniel Anderson for his comments in this connection. For more on this topic see Ian Watt, *Conrad in the Nineteenth Century*, Berkeley/Los Angeles: University of California Press, 1979, pp. 161-168.

[83] *Lord Jim*, p. 38.
[84] *Lord Jim*, p. 202.

[85] James, *The Briefer Course*, p. 297.

[86] *Lord Jim*, p. 125. A nice emblem, this mannerism, of the rupture in the soul that makes Jim to be Jim in the first place!

[87] *The Heart of Darkness*.

[88] I already speak of "the restored position" even though, strictly speaking,

my account of Jim thus far is still a few negations shy of establishing this. For an in-depth discussion of the four moments of the dialectic of sublation (initial position, negation, negation of the negation, and the restored position) see Wolfgang Giegerich, David L. Miller, Greg Mogenson, *Dialectics & Analytical Psychology: The El Capitan Canyon Seminar*, New Orleans: Spring Journal Books, 2005, pp. 1-24, 77-106.

[89] In his song, "Gotta Serve Somebody," Bob Dylan lists all manner of roles one may have in life—businessman, rock'n' roll star, doctor, boxer, ambassador, etc., interspersing these with the constant refrain, "But you're going to have to serve somebody." Especially pertinent in the present context is the line stating that "you may be living in another country under another name / But your gonna have to serve somebody …"

[90] *Lord Jim*, p. 125.

[91] About such dreams, Jung writes, "… behind the impressions of daily life—behind the scenes—another picture looms up, covered by a thin veil of actual facts" (*The Visions Seminars*, Book One, Zürich: Spring Publications, 1976, p. 8). Although I spoke of being "tasked with a strange, and yet, defining adventure," this needs to be tempered with an understanding of the just as important need to distinguish ourselves from the soul, i.e., to eschew the inflation that identification with such images may inspire. This, I find, may often be achieved by regarding the imagery less as a task that is yet to be achieved than as the reflection of an already existing situation seen from within. For further comments on this topic, which also draws upon this text of Jung's, see Giegerich, *Neurosis: The Logic of a Metaphysical Illness*, pp. 176-177, fn. 118.

[92] Immanuel Kant, *The Critique of Practical Reason*, "Conclusion" section.

[93] To Ewald Jung, 31 July, 1935. In Jung, *Letters*, vol. I, p. 193. My italics.

[94] Jung's statement about our "*appear[ing] wondrously strange to ourselves*" may be read in relation to another of his texts: "If this supra-individual psyche exists, everything that is translated into its picture-language would be depersonalized, and if this became conscious would appear to us *sub specie aeternitatis*. Not as my sorrow, but as the sorrow of the world; not as personal isolating pain, but a pain without bitterness that units all humanity. The healing effect of this needs no proof" (*CW* 8 § 316).

95 In his "Commentary to 'The Secret of the Golden Flower'," Jung writes: "A growing familiarity with the spirit of the East should be taken merely as a sign that we are beginning to relate to the alien elements within ourselves" (*CW* 13 § 72). See also Jung's statement with respect to the "unexpectedly dark brother" which the European meets in his travels to North Africa, India, etc.: "and though I deny it a thousand times, *it is also in me*" (*CW* 18 § 1472).

96 The exotic Jewel's fierce and uncanny love for Jim beautifully exemplifies what Jung theorized as the compensating role of the anima with respect to the persona, or in our context, with respect to the persona-field (*CW* 6 § 803). This motif comes up frequently in analytic work. A patient, for example, speaks out passionately at a public meeting about a controversial issue. Immediately he realizes that it has not gone over well. Apologies are subsequently demanded, his resignation, too. But then, in the midst of his demoralized state, he dreams that he is a young man "singing his song" in a seedy, out-of-the-way tavern, where *he is befriended by a young woman* whom he recalls as having been an especially interesting and enthusiastic student of his during his first year as a professor.

97 *Lord Jim*, pp. 207-208.

98 Jung, *Letters*, vol. 2, August 1956, to H. A. Murray, p. 324. Cited by Giegerich, *CEP*, vol. III, p. 75.

99 Aniela Jaffé, "The Individuation of Mankind," in her *Was C. G. Jung a Mystic?*, Einsiedeln: Daimon Verlag, 1989, pp. 53-102.

100 Cf. Jung, "Whenever there exists some external form, be it an ideal or a ritual, by which all the yearnings and hopes of the soul are adequately expressed—as for instance in a living religion—then we may say the psyche is outside and there is no psychic problem, just as there is then no unconscious in our sense of the word. In consonance with this truth, the discovery of psychology falls entirely within the last decades, although long before that man was introspective and intelligent enough to recognize the facts that are the subject-matter of psychology" (*CW* 10 § 159).

101 This difference between the psychic and the psychological, or again, between the empirically human, on the one hand, and the shared values, meanings, and truths of Man's world relation, on the other, is sharply drawn in the novel when a French naval officer with whom Marlow discusses the case of Jim states that although man is born a coward honour is a reality

that must be upheld (*Lord Jim*, p. 152). For Giegerich's introduction of the term "psychological difference" into the discourse of analytical psychology see his "The Present as a Dimension of the Soul: 'Actual Conflict' and Archetypal Psychology," *CEP*, vol. I, pp. 111-112.

[102] Giegerich, "The End of Meaning and the Birth of Man," in *CEP*, vol. IV, pp. 189-284.

[103] G. W. F. Hegel, *The Science of Logic*, George Di Giovanni, trans., Cambridge: Cambridge University Press, 2010, p. 81.

[104] This figure of Hegel's may be read in relation to Jung's statement: "any judgment and any statement about [the self] is incomplete and has to be supplemented (but not nullified) by a conditioned negative. If I assert, 'The self exists,' I must supplement this by saying, 'But it seems not to exist.' For the sake of completeness I must also invert the proposition and say, 'the self does not exist, but yet seems to exist'" (*CW* 11 § 399n).

[105] Hegel, *Phenomenology of Spirit*, § 25, 37, pp. 14, 21.

[106] I say, "determinately negated," with Hegel's concept of determinate negation in mind. When something, here Duty, is contradicted or negated, it does not simply become nothing at all, but continues in a subtle (i.e., logically negative) manner to impart itself upon the successor situation as a sublated moment within it. Likewise, my descriptive phrase, "kenotically repurposed," draws upon the concept of *kenôsis* which in Paul's "Letter to the Philippians" (2:5-8) has do to with Christ's humbling himself and giving up his divinity in the course of an incarnation process which culminates in his human death upon the cross. My aim is to imply something similar with respect to Duty as a truth of those traditional times that were coming to an end in the period in which our novel is set. For a discussion of *kenôsis* from the psychological angle see Giegerich, "God Must Not Die! Jung's Thesis of the One-sidedness of Christianity," in *CEP*, vol. VI, pp. 199-208.

[107] On the topic of finding into one's own truth, a passage from Giegerich is worth quoting. Using Jung's statement "I am *only* that!" as a figure for one's emancipation from the soul, he writes: "When I am '*only* that,' I am without higher orders, even without the mythical garment of an endowment (be it by Nature or by the Creator) with the 'dignity of man' or 'inalienable human rights,' these inflated modern ideas. I cannot bask in the shine of an eternal truth, an absolute ideal, or higher values that would be in my possession. No such thing has revealed itself to me and claimed me. And yet, this does by no

means mean that 'anything goes.' I am not without truth, norms, values. But they conversely receive their authority and reality only from *my* being-so and *my* standing up for them. In this sense, they are fundamentally contingent, subjective: human, all-too-human; there is no essential difference to my liking this food or art or music and disliking that. What gives them their objectivity is the objective fact of my being-so." To this he adds: "Certain things, views, possible behaviours, etc., happen to be incompatible with who and how I am. *This* is the only 'proof' I can offer for my truths. Here I stand, I cannot do otherwise. But here I *do* stand, and really *stand*." Giegerich, "The End of Meaning and the Birth of Man," in *CEP*, vol. IV, p. 237.

[108] Psychology, of course, in the sense intended here, began as a treatment for neurosis. Productive of one another (!), these, it can be said, came hand in hand as the successors of the religion and tradition that preceded them. Highly illustrative of this relation is another of Conrad's novels of the sea, *The Nigger of the 'Narcissus.'* In that novel (as I read it), Duty meets a figure of its negation in the character of a black sailor who is exempted from his work due to a sickness that is often thought to be—though this is never clear—a matter of malingering. Anticipating our own time of rights, entitlements, and special accommodations (we may think here, for example, of the across the board extensions that are now granted to anxious university and college students at exam time), his individualistic needs are asserted through the symptoms of his illness, as dubious as these are. Mutinous tensions build up amongst the crew, inspired by their identification with his plight. The ideal of Duty, which was never questioned by Jim in the novel about him, gives way before concerns about their rights and entitlements as individuals. And along with this, a cowardly denial of death reflects the decline of the traditional belief in the immortality of the soul, which had previously been the backbone of good conduct and character.

[109] *Lord Jim*, p. 303.
[110] *Lord Jim*, p. 324.
[111] *Lord Jim*, p. 328.

[112] Jim's shame before Captain Brown, who personifies the plundering spirit of the colonialist powers of that period, shows that he did not fully grasp the truth of which he was the pioneer. Many of Jim's lasting critics would not credit his achievements among the Malay, since in their view "'giving your life up for them' (*them* meaning all of mankind with skins brown, yellow, or black in colour) 'was like selling your soul to a brute.'" Against this view, Marlow contends that Jim's valuing and being valued by the

Malay, his making his life among them and finding his opportunity through them, was the basis of his life's "message to an impeccable world." *Lord Jim*, p. 293.

[113] *Lord Jim*, p. 200.

[114] For a presentation of an attitude that is more in keeping with the "going under" that is here described see James Hillman's essay, "Three Ways of Failure and Analysis," in *Loose Ends: Primary Papers in Archetypal Psychology*, Irving, Texas: Spring Publications, 1978, pp. 98-104.

[115] *Lord Jim*, p. 202.

[116] The Beautiful Soul refers to that kind of subjectivity and personhood that, clinging to the ideals of its illusory self-identicalness, withdraws into itself in flight from the negations which its world metes out. For a thoroughgoing analysis of conscience, duty, and the problem of the Beautiful Soul see Hegel, *Phenomenology of Spirit*, § 632-671, pp. 383-409.

[117] *Lord Jim*, p. 304.

[118] Jung, *Memories, Dreams, Reflections*, p. 171. For a thoroughgoing discussion of this faulty dialectic see Giegerich, "The Flight into the Unconscious: C. G. Jung's Psychology Project," *CEP*, vol. V, pp. 177-192.

[119] *Lord Jim*, p. 329.
[120] *Lord Jim*, p. 329

[121] Brown is no less a mediating figure with respect to the dialectic that Duty is subject to in the novel than are Jim, Captain Brierly, Marlow, and the other characters. For further insight into what might be called his tautegorical necessity in this regard, comparison may be drawn to a statement of Hegel's about how nonsense and crime can serve to bring out the effeteness and untruth of the values of a society. Writing with respect to the infinite negative judgment, which is exemplified in nonsense, on the one hand, and crime on the other, Hegel states that this "... must not be considered merely as a contingent form of subjective thinking; [since] on the contrary, *it shows itself to be the proximate dialectical result of the preceding immediate judgments (the positive and the simply negative), whose finitude and untruth come to light explicitly in it.*" G.W. F. Hegel, *The Encyclopaedia Logic (with the Zusätze): Part 1 of the Encyclopaedia of the Philosophic Sciences with Zusätze*, § 173, p. 251, italics mine. For more elucidation of this topic see my *Psychology's*

Dream of the Courtroom, New Orleans: Spring Journal Book, 2016, pp. 155-168, 174-193. For more on what I here referred to as "tautegorical necessity," see Giegerich's discussion of "The 'tautological' presupposition of myth interpretation" in his *The Soul's Logical Life*, pp. 119-123.

[122] Looking a little more deeply into the dialectic that is depicted here, it is helpful to realize that from the soul's point of view such violence is only a means of presenting a change of consciousness. Just as we say, "the truth hurts," such violent scenes are only the first immediacy of the realization that things are not what they had been thought to be. It is because a truth that is no longer true is being conservatively adhered to that consciousness or "the soul" dirempts itself into Jim, on the one hand, and Captain Brown, on the other. Such a diremption, however, is no longer necessary for a consciousness that has followed through with the determinately negative repurposing of duty from which the psychological age emerged. Of this I will give one representative example. In his 1845 book, *The Ego and His Own: The Case of the Individual Against Authority* (New York: Verso, 2014), Max Stirner, already leaving the concerns of Jim far behind, resolutely declares his emancipation from the soul: "If god, if mankind, ... have substance enough in themselves to be all in all to themselves, then I feel that *I* shall still less lack that, and that I shall have no complaint to make of my 'emptiness.' I am not nothing in the sense of emptiness, but I am the creative nothing, the nothing out which I myself as creator create everything. ... The divine is God's concern; the human, man's. My concern is neither the divine nor the human, not the true, good, just, free, etc., but solely what is *mine*, and it is not a general one, but is—unique, as I am unique. Nothing is more to me than myself!" (p. xxiii). Compare here Hegel's aforementioned "Speculative Remark" about how sublatedness is to be distinguished from nothing in that it has its origin in a something that has gone under into it, i.e., into the form of logically negativity.

[123] *Lord Jim*, p. 345.
[124] *Lord Jim*, p. 351.
[125] *Lord Jim*, p. 351.

ABOUT THE AUTHOR

Greg Mogenson is a registered psychotherapist and Jungian psycho-analyst practicing in London, Ontario, Canada. He is the editor of The Studies in Archetypal Psychology Series of Spring Journal Books as well as a founding member and Vice-President of The International Society for Psychology as the Discipline of Interiority. The author of numerous articles in the field of analytical psychology, his books include *Psychology's Dream of the Courtroom; A Most Accursed Religion: When a Trauma becomes God; Greeting the Angels: An Imaginal View of the Mourning Process; The Dove in the Consulting Room: Hysteria and the Anima in Bollas and Jung; Northern Gnosis: Thor, Baldr, and the Volsungs in the Thought of Freud and Jung,* and (with W. Giegerich and D. L. Miller) *Dialectics & Analytical Psychology: The El Capitan Canyon Seminar.*

For further information, visit the website at: www.gregmogenson.com